❦ History *of* Britain ❦

Tudor Explorers

Brian Williams

Illustrated by Mark Bergin

HAMLYN

HISTORY OF BRITAIN –TUDOR EXPLORERS
was produced for Hamlyn Children's Books
by Lionheart Books, London
Editor: Lionel Bender
Designer: Ben White
Editorial Assistant: Madeleine Samuel, Jo Hanks
Picture Researcher: Jennie Karrach
Media Conversion and Typesetting:
  Peter MacDonald
Educational Consultant: Jane Shuter
Editorial Advisors: Andrew Farrow, Paul Shuter
Production Controller: Catherine Bald
Editorial Director: David Riley

First published in Great Britain in 1995
by Hamlyn Children's Books,
an imprint of Reed International Books,
Michelin House, 81 Fulham Road, London SW3 6RB,
and Auckland, Melbourne, Singapore and Toronto.

ISBN 0 600 58782 7 Hb   ISBN 0 600 58783 5 Pb
British Library Cataloguing-in-Publication Data.
A catalogue record for this book is available
from the British Library.
Printed in China

Acknowledgements
All illustrations by Mark Bergin except maps, by
Hayward Art Group.
Picture credits
BAL = The Bridgeman Art Library, NPG = By courtesy of
the National Portrait Gallery, London, MC = The Mansell
Collection.
l = left, r = right, t = top, b = bottom, c = centre.
Pages: 4t: Anthony Blake Photo Library. 5t: Biblioteca
Estense ed Universitaria di Modena, Italy/Foto Roncaglia.
5b: BAL/City of Bristol Museum & Art Gallery. 6tr: NPG.
6cl: Michael Holford. 7: MC. 8b: BAL/National Maritime
Museum, London. 9: By Courtesy of the Master and
Fellows of Magdalene College, Cambridge. 10: Plymouth
City Museums & Art Gallery Collection. 11t: Hispanic·
Society of America. 11b: Werner Forman Archive. 12l:
Bodleian Library, Oxford. 13t, 13c: BAL/By Courtesy of
the Trustees of the British Museum, London. 13b: With the
Permission of the Marquess of Salisbury, Hatfield House.
14bl: Fotomas Index. 14tr: NPG. 15t: Fotomas Index.
15c: e.t. archive. 16bl: Fotomas Index. 16cr: BAL/New
York Public Library. 17tl: Fotomas Index. 17cr: By
Courtesy of the Master and Fellows of Magdalene College,
Cambridge. 18tl, 18tr: BAL/By Courtesy of the Trustees
of the British Museum, London. 18br: NPG. 19t: BAL/By
Courtesy of the Trustees of the British Museum, London.
19b: MC. 20t: NPG. 20b: Pierpont Morgan Library/Art
Resource/MA 3900. f.97. 21t: Drake Print – Hulton
Deutsch. 21b: MC. 22tr: Historical Society of
Pennsylvania. 22bl: BAL/By Courtesy of the Trustees of
the British Museum, London.
Cover: Artwork by Mark Bergin. Icons by Michael Shoebridge.
Photos: (Frobisher's second voyage & Virginia Colony): BAL/
By Courtesy of the Trustees of the British Museum, London.
(Portrait of Drake): NPG. (English raid): Hulton Deutsch.

PLACES TO VISIT

Here are some museums and sites connected with Tudor
Explorers you can visit, with treasures, statues of famous
seamen, ships and paintings of the time to see.

Berkeley Castle, Gloucestershire. Oak chest from Drake's
cabin on board the *Golden Hind* on its round-the-world
voyage.

Bristol, Avon. Seaport city, with historic trade links with
America. Museum with items from America. A monument
on Brandon Hill commemorates John Cabot.

Buckland Abbey, Devon. Home of Grenville and Drake, now
a museum; banners flown on board the *Golden Hind*.

Burghley House, Huntingdon. Great Tudor mansion, home of
the Cecil family from 1587.

Hampton Court, Surrey. Royal palace, with a great hall built
for King Henry VIII.

Hatfield House, Hertfordshire. House owned by the Cecils,
on the site of a royal palace where Elizabeth lived before
she was queen. Has examples of Raleigh's writings.

National Maritime Museum, Greenwich, London. Pictures,
maps, models and items from ships of the time. Exhibits
include Drake's Dial, his world map and medal.

National Portrait Gallery, London. Paintings of English
leaders and sea captains of the time, including Raleigh.

Plymouth, Devon. Port from which many voyages began.
Museum exhibits include a cup given to Drake by Queen
Elizabeth I.

Portsmouth, Hampshire. Tudor warship *Mary Rose*, restored
and displayed with items found on board to show what life
at sea was like in the mid-1500s.

Tavistock, Devon. Drake's birthplace, and a statue in his
honour.

INTRODUCTION

At the end of the 1400s the Portuguese and Spanish began exploring oceans and lands previously unknown to Europeans. Their ships sailed round Africa to India, and across the Atlantic Ocean to America. English, French and Dutch sailors soon followed, and so began a century of exploration. Throughout the 1500s Europeans explored the new, wider world that was opening up before them. Merchants sought new trade routes. Sailors mapped new seas. Soldiers fought and conquered for gold and silver. Colonists went in search of new lands to settle. The people of Tudor England, ruled by monarchs from Henry VII to Elizabeth I, played a growing part in this adventure.

CONTENTS

A Wider World

The voyages of Columbus to America (1492) and Magellan round the world (1519-21) proved that the world was larger than Europeans thought. Traders were eager to explore the new lands, hoping to find riches greater even than those of Asia.

In 1522, one ship with 18 seamen left on board returned to Spain. Five ships had set out. The men's leader, Ferdinand Magellan, was dead. They had become the first people to sail round the world.

Europeans, and the Catholic Church, had already divided the 'New World' as if they owned it. By 1540 Spain had seized Mexico and much of South America. Portugal controlled the trade routes by sea round Africa to India, China and Japan. English merchants had to look elsewhere for overseas trade. They hoped to profit from John Cabot's voyages to America.

△ **Spices from Asia, such as pepper and ginger**, were used in Europe to make dried or salted meat and fish more tasty. To bring them overland to Europe took two years. Spices fetched a high price so were worth a risky voyage.

▷ **Some of the great voyages of exploration from western Europe.**
● The Portuguese sailed around Africa. By this route, Vasco da Gama reached India in 1498.
● Columbus and Cabot sailed west across the Atlantic Ocean to 'discover' America.
● Magellan's sailors circled the world.
● The Spaniards Cortés and Pizarro explored parts of Central and South America.
● Jacques Cartier of France landed in Canada.

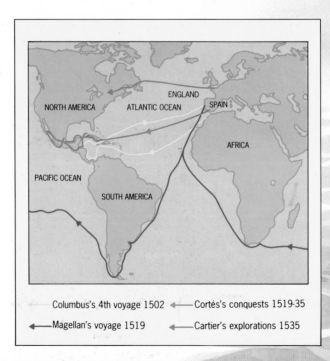

NORTH AMERICA
ENGLAND
ATLANTIC OCEAN
SPAIN
AFRICA
PACIFIC OCEAN
SOUTH AMERICA

Columbus's 4th voyage 1502 ← ← Cortés's conquests 1519-35
← Magellan's voyage 1519 ← Cartier's explorations 1535

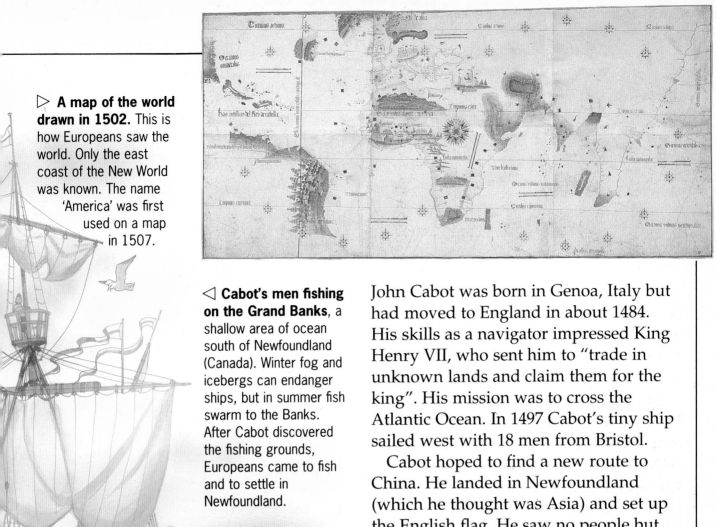

▷ **A map of the world drawn in 1502.** This is how Europeans saw the world. Only the east coast of the New World was known. The name 'America' was first used on a map in 1507.

◁ **Cabot's men fishing on the Grand Banks**, a shallow area of ocean south of Newfoundland (Canada). Winter fog and icebergs can endanger ships, but in summer fish swarm to the Banks. After Cabot discovered the fishing grounds, Europeans came to fish and to settle in Newfoundland.

John Cabot was born in Genoa, Italy but had moved to England in about 1484. His skills as a navigator impressed King Henry VII, who sent him to "trade in unknown lands and claim them for the king". His mission was to cross the Atlantic Ocean. In 1497 Cabot's tiny ship sailed west with 18 men from Bristol.

Cabot hoped to find a new route to China. He landed in Newfoundland (which he thought was Asia) and set up the English flag. He saw no people but discovered the rich fishing grounds of the Grand Banks, where cod could be caught by the basketful. However, the English were disappointed to find no spices, gold or wealthy cities.

John Cabot set out again in 1498, with five ships. What happened to them is a mystery as no ships returned.

◁ **Sebastian Cabot** (about 1476-1557). He was King Henry VIII's mapmaker. He may have sailed with his father John (about 1450-1499) on the first English voyage to America. Sebastian wanted to find a 'Northeast Passage' to Asia, through Arctic waters north of Norway.

5

NEW ROUTES TO THE EAST

In 1500 England was no match for Spain or Portugal at sea. But by the 1550s it had a growing navy and a fleet of trading ships. Merchants paying for these ships' voyages wanted to find new trade routes to Asia, free from the influence of Spain or Portugal.

English merchants were eager to buy and sell in Asia. But the old trade route to Asia, by ship across the Mediterranean Sea and then overland through the Middle East, was beset by dangers from pirates and raiders.

▷ **Queen Elizabeth I** wanted to avoid war with Spain. But she was willing to pay for English ships to trade, take slaves and raid Spanish treasure ships.

▽ **Explorers sought a Northeast Passage**, a sea route to Asia round Scandinavia and Russia. (Left, a scene from Asia.) The Arctic seas are mostly frozen, and no Tudor ship could make such a voyage.
● Englishmen Willoughby, Chancellor and Stephen Borough, and Dutch explorer Willem Barents (about 1550-1597), all failed in their attempts to find the Northeast Passage.

There was another route from Europe to Asia – the long sea voyage round Africa and across the Indian Ocean. It was the way Portuguese sailors had reached India, the East Indies and Japan.

By the 1550s the Portuguese had warships and coastal forts along this route to stop any rivals stealing their trade. So the English looked for a new way to Asia.

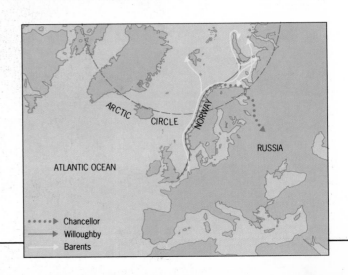

ARCTIC CIRCLE

NORWAY

RUSSIA

ATLANTIC OCEAN

•••••▶ Chancellor
——▶ Willoughby
——— Barents

◁ **Drawing of a wealthy merchant's warehouse in about 1535.** Trading voyages were risky, for a merchant's ships might be lost at sea. But a successful voyage could make him rich. Merchants formed companies to share the risks and profits of trade voyages. The Merchant Adventurers controlled English cloth sales abroad. The Muscovy (Moscow) Company was started in 1555 to trade with Russia.

Merchants sent sailors to explore the northern seas, to look for an ice-free 'passage' to Asia. In 1553 Sir Hugh Willoughby and Richard Chancellor set out with three ships to sail round Norway to "Cathay (China) and other regions, dominions, islands and places unknown". A violent storm separated Chancellor's ship from the other two, which soon became frozen in the Arctic ice. Willoughby and his companions died from cold and lack of food, but Chancellor's ship reached the north coast of Russia. He and his crew then trekked overland to Moscow, where they met the Russian emperor, Ivan IV. Ivan welcomed trade with England, and the Muscovy (Moscow) Company was set up to run it.

▷ **Captain Richard Chancellor meets Ivan the Terrible, the Russian tsar (emperor).** 'Terrible' meant 'awesome', though Ivan could be brutal too. The tsar welcomed the English visitors, and agreed to give English merchants trade privileges.

SHIPS TO SAIL THE WORLD

During the Middle Ages ship design changed little, but from 1500 to 1600 bigger and faster ships were built in Europe. These new ships could sail across oceans. They were armed with cannon to fight rivals and conquer weaker peoples.

Columbus's biggest ship, the *Santa Maria*, was only 26 metres long and weighed about 80 tonnes. By the 1550s European shipbuilders were launching ships weighing hundreds of tonnes. The new ships had three or four masts, carrying both square sails and triangular sails. They sailed well in light or strong winds, and were more easily steered than older ships. Known as galleons, the new ships could both trade and fight.

The sailors lived in the bow (front) of the ship, beneath the raised 'forecastle'. The captain and officers had cabins in the sterncastle, at the rear. Cannon were ranged along the upper decks. The sailors were armed with muskets, swords, daggers, pikes, bows and clubs. They were ready to fight pirates, rival traders or the people in the new lands they explored.

Bow

▽ **All sailors, or mariners, had hard lives.** They risked death from disease or drowning, and often had only rotten food and bad water. Seamen did not wear uniforms. They wore thick working clothes like these, to keep as warm as possible.

▽ **To find their way, seamen used navigation instruments** like this astrolabe which belonged to Francis Drake. The navigator measured the Sun's angle above the horizon. Using tables, he could work out how far north or south of the equator he was, and also the time.

8

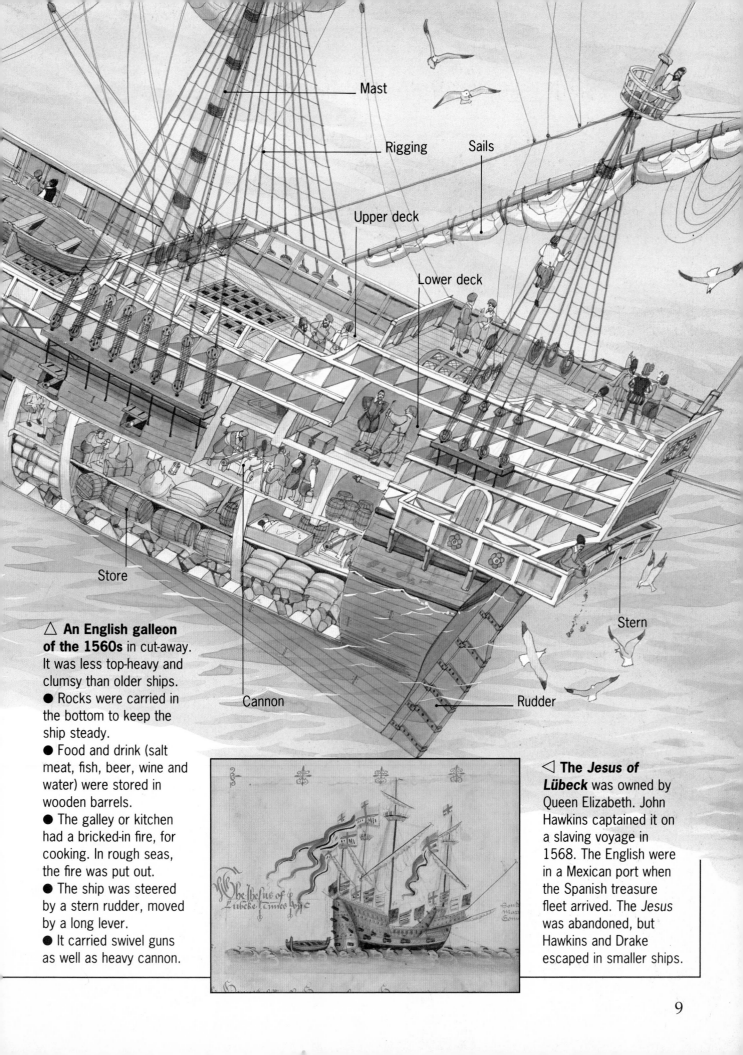

Mast

Rigging   Sails

Upper deck

Lower deck

Store

Cannon

Stern

Rudder

△ **An English galleon of the 1560s** in cut-away. It was less top-heavy and clumsy than older ships.
● Rocks were carried in the bottom to keep the ship steady.
● Food and drink (salt meat, fish, beer, wine and water) were stored in wooden barrels.
● The galley or kitchen had a bricked-in fire, for cooking. In rough seas, the fire was put out.
● The ship was steered by a stern rudder, moved by a long lever.
● It carried swivel guns as well as heavy cannon.

◁ **The *Jesus of Lübeck*** was owned by Queen Elizabeth. John Hawkins captained it on a slaving voyage in 1568. The English were in a Mexican port when the Spanish treasure fleet arrived. The *Jesus* was abandoned, but Hawkins and Drake escaped in smaller ships.

SLAVES AND GOLD

In their American Empire, the Spanish forced the Indians to work. When they needed more workers, they bought slaves from Africa. English ships carried many of these slaves, who were exchanged for American goods.

Selling slaves gave the English a chance to trade in America. The Spanish killed thousands of American Indians and many died from overwork or disease. English interest in the slave trade began in 1562 when John Hawkins sailed to Sierra Leone in West Africa. He collected 300 slaves from local traders, and took them to the Spanish island of Hispaniola in the Caribbean, where he sold them.

▽ **John Hawkins (1532-1595).** From slave trading, he went on to direct the rebuilding of the English fleet. Later he fought the Spanish Armada.

▷ **A Spanish mine in America.** Tales of America's wealth, like the 'silver mountain' found at Potosi in Peru in 1545, excited the English too. When treasure fleets sailed for Spain, English ships were waiting to rob them. Spain complained about English piracy, but Queen Elizabeth I did nothing to stop her seamen's raids.

Slave voyages were profitable. Queen Elizabeth privately lent Hawkins ships and money for a second voyage in 1564. If Spanish officials in America argued with Hawkins about prices, he sent his sailors and soldiers ashore to settle the dispute. If the English met a Portuguese ship off the coast of Africa, they would seize the cargo and sell it to the Spanish in America.

English ships also raided Spanish treasure ships, carrying gold and silver from America to Spain. This angered Spain, and in 1568 the Spanish attacked Hawkins' fleet in the Mexican port of San Juan de Ulua. Hawkins lost his own ship and many men, but still brought home chests of gold, silver and pearls.

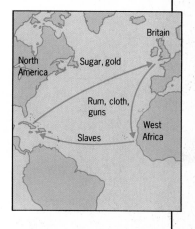

◁ **Hawkins and his men inspect slaves** on a beach in West Africa. The slaves were taken by rowing boats to the ship and crammed inside for the voyage to America.

▷ **A bronze figure of European traders**, made by an African artist in West Africa in the 1580s.

△ **The slave trade** was one side of a 'trade triangle'. Europeans sailed to Africa with rum, cloth, metal goods and guns. They sold these to local traders in exchange for slaves. In America the slaves were sold to the Spanish merchants in exchange for sugar and gold, which were brought back to Europe.

11

THE NORTHWESTERN VOYAGERS

The search for a new sea route to Asia was a challenge for the bravest seafarers. English ships steered north into Arctic waters, looking for new oceans and lands to claim. These were brave, but unsuccessful, attempts to find a Northwest Passage.

Magellan had sailed south round America, and found a sea channel joining the Atlantic and Pacific oceans. Other navigators expected to discover a similar channel to the north of America or Russia. It would be a shorter route to Asia, and well clear of the Spanish and Portuguese.

In 1576 Martin Frobisher sailed from London, and got as far as Baffin Land, north of Canada. None of the inlets he explored led to Asia, but he found some shiny rocks, which he believed to be gold.

△ **Martin Frobisher (about 1536-1594).** He made three Arctic voyages, but failed in his plan to start an English colony in North America. In 1588 he helped to lead the English fleet against the Armada.

▷ **Trapped in the ice.** John Davis (about 1550-1605) led three Arctic voyages. Although they were ill-equipped for polar exploring, his men were resourceful. They cut ice to stop the ship freezing in Arctic waters.

Encouraged by Elizabeth I, Frobisher led 15 ships to Canada in 1578. He hoped to start a colony. But the shiny rocks proved to be iron, and the land was too barren for his settlers. They came home disappointed. In 1578 Sir Humphrey Gilbert also tried to find the Northwest Passage. He lost his best ship, but tried again in 1583. This time he planned to start a North American colony. One ship sank, with 100 colonists, and the other two ships sailed for home. Gilbert's ship sank, and he was drowned.

Sailing among Arctic ice and fog was hazardous. The North Magnetic Pole made ships' compasses unreliable. Only the most skilful seamen could hope to return. John Davis made three Arctic voyages, in 1585, 1586 and 1587. He explored the coast of Greenland, and met the Inuit people of the Arctic islands. Later he discovered the Falkland Islands. In 1605 Davis was killed by pirates in the East Indies.

△ **An unfriendly meeting with Inuit (Eskimos)**, drawn by an English artist in the 1580s. Frobisher's men fought off this attack during their second voyage to Baffin Island in 1577. When ice around the Arctic islands blocked their ships, the English used rowing boats. Believing he had found gold in Labrador, Frobisher gave up the search for a Northwest Passage to China.

◁ **An Inuit woman** as drawn by English colonist John White in 1580.

◁ **Map used by Martin Frobisher** in his search for the Northwest Passage. It shows navigation lines and some of the coastline of the British Isles and Norway.

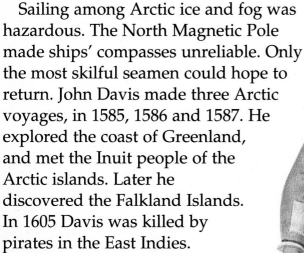

DRAKE AROUND THE WORLD

An American Indian in Panama told the Spanish explorer Balboa in 1513 that there was another sea where ships as big as Balboa's could sail. Balboa was the first European to see the Pacific Ocean, and the Spanish claimed it as their territory. In 1577 the English set sail to explore this vast ocean themselves.

Only a few people in England knew that one of their captains was preparing, as the geographer John Dee wrote "...to accomplish that discovery which many captains have often attempted in vain".

Geographers wanted to know if Asia and America were joined. Or was there a sea channel between the north Atlantic and the north Pacific? Was there a large southern continent, as yet unknown?

Most seamen were more interested in Spanish gold. Francis Drake and John Oxenham had crossed Spanish Panama in 1573, and seen the Pacific. On a second land raid in 1576-1577, Oxenham was captured and executed by the Spanish. Now the English planned a voyage into and across the Pacific, and onwards round the world.

▽ **Drake's voyage round the world.** It was nearly three years before Drake (right) and the crew of the *Golden Hind* returned to England.

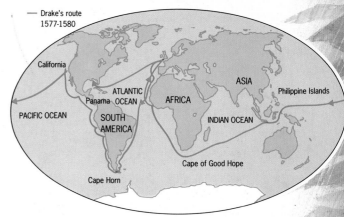

— Drake's route 1577-1580

◁ **Title page of a book for seamen**, dedicated to Drake. On his voyage Drake took three navigation books, one by Magellan. He had maps, but also captured local fishermen and traders as pilots (guides). Drake kept careful notes of the voyage and drew pictures of the plants and animals he saw.

Francis Drake was to lead the expedition. He was given five ships and about 200 men. His secret orders were to look for a southern continent, set up trade agreements in Asia, and raid Spanish ships and bases. Queen Elizabeth secretly gave Drake her support. England was not at war with Spain, but Spanish gold was tempting.

Drake left Plymouth for South America in December 1577. Off Africa, he captured several ships as well as a sailor who knew the coast of Brazil and would be useful as a navigator.

△ **A Tudor world map made after Drake's voyage.** His own ship, the *Pelican*, was renamed *Golden Hind* by Drake. It carried 18 guns, weighed about 100 tonnes and was 21 metres long. Of the five ships, only the *Golden Hind* (right) circled the world.

◁ **Drake's ships are battered by stormy seas in the Pacific.** Three of the ships sailed round South America. Then they were scattered by gales. The *Marigold* sank. The *Elizabeth* turned for home. Drake sailed north. Giving up hope of meeting his companions, he went on alone to attack Spanish settlements in Peru.

CALIFORNIA AND THE PACIFIC

Drake promised his crew riches, but he told his officers and sailors that they must share the hardships ahead. Magellan took four months to cross the Pacific. To survive, his crew had eaten leather sail-covers, sawdust and rats.

As he cruised off the coast of Spanish America, Drake prepared to raid the Spanish. He moved fast, attacking the port of Lima in Peru. There he learned that a Spanish silver-ship, the *Cacafuego*, had left Panama. He sped north, ahead of two pursuing Spanish ships, and seized this rich prize.

Now loaded with plunder, he decided not to risk a land raid on Panama. Off the coast of Nicaragua, Drake captured two local seamen. They gave him maps to guide him across the Pacific, which no English seamen had ever crossed. In Mexico, his men filled the ship's barrels with fresh water. Then instead of crossing the ocean, the *Golden Hind* sailed north to California.

▽ **Francis Drake** was the first English explorer to set foot here on the west coast of South America. In 1579, he set up a sign claiming California for England. A brass plate declaring this was found near Drake's Bay, California, in 1937. It may be the original plate.

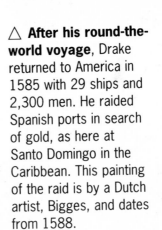

△ **After his round-the-world voyage**, Drake returned to America in 1585 with 29 ships and 2,300 men. He raided Spanish ports in search of gold, as here at Santo Domingo in the Caribbean. This painting of the raid is by a Dutch artist, Bigges, and dates from 1588.

▷ **In California, Drake is greeted by friendly Indians.** The English landed near San Francisco Bay in June 1579. They stayed a month, beaching their ship for cleaning and repairs before the Pacific crossing. Drake claimed the Indians' land for Queen Elizabeth.

16

▽ **This is Drake's own map, showing the British Isles, France and Spain.** The English Channel was where Drake and his seamen learned navigation.

△ **The heavily armed *Golden Hind* was a match for any Spanish ship in the Americas.** Drake's most valuable prize was the treasure ship *Cacafuego* (above). English tactics were to fire at an enemy ship, then board, often from small boats. Drake's men took any gold and silver, but usually let the ship and its crew sail away.

Caca Fogo.   *Caca Plata.*

Drake may have been looking for a Pacific outlet of the Northwest Passage, and a short-cut home. He did not find one, but he was able to repair his ship, safe from Spanish pursuit. At the end of July 1579 he left America, and by September he had reached Polynesia. As the year ended, he was buying cloves in the Molucca Islands (Indonesia).

In January 1580 the *Golden Hind* struck a rock. The crew threw half the cloves and two guns overboard to refloat the ship. Drake visited Java, and then sailed east across the Indian Ocean. He rounded the tip of Africa, landed in Sierra Leone for water and fresh food, and was back home in Plymouth on 26 September 1580. News of his raids had reached Europe, and Spain demanded the return of its silver.

In England, the 'master thief of the unknown world' was welcomed as a hero, and Queen Elizabeth knighted Drake in 1581.

THE FIRST COLONISTS

Drake brought huge profits to his English backers. But Spain was still in control of South America. North America offered more freedom for English explorers and settlers. Some went looking for gold. Others hoped to start new lives. The first attempts at settlement went badly, but people kept trying.

△ **An American Indian**, drawn by John White. The Indians at first helped the English.

◁ **An Indian village** as drawn by colonist John White on his first visit to America in 1585. In America, the English saw strange animals and plants. Turkeys, tobacco and potatoes were all new to them. The Indians showed the English how to grow maize (sweetcorn). Walter Raleigh (shown below with his son) helped set up the first colonies.

The English began by trying to set up settlements on the east coast of what is now the United States. Such 'colonies' offered adventure, trade, and freedom for people seeking to escape poverty or religious persecution at home.

Sir Walter Raleigh was a soldier and courtier, and a favourite of Elizabeth I. He paid for two ships to sail to Roanoke Island, in modern North Carolina. The sailors found grapes growing, and the Indians friendly. So in 1585, 100 colonists and soldiers landed there. But they could not grow enough crops to survive. Also, the soldiers quarrelled with the Indians. When Drake, on a raiding voyage, arrived to seek supplies, the colonists sailed home with him.

△ **An Indian woman and child, also drawn by John White.** The settlers were not helpless – Tudor men and women had many skills, and many of the colonists were well armed. But they faced a hard struggle in a strange land.

◁ **Unloading stores on Roanoke Island in 1587.** There were 91 men, 17 women and 9 children in the party, led by John White. They built log houses and a fort. Three years later White came back to find his friends had vanished.

In the summer of 1587 Raleigh sent a second large expedition to Roanoke. A month later their leader, John White, sailed to England for supplies. But Raleigh was now short of money, and England was about to fight the Spanish Armada. By the time White was able to return to America in 1590, the colonists had disappeared.

The English had learned that settlers must be able to grow their own food and make the things they needed. In 1607 a new English colony was founded at Jamestown, Virginia. Its leader was John Smith. The colonists bought corn from the Indians and learned to grow tobacco, which they sold to England. These settlers had come to stay.

▽ **Pocahontas** was the daughter of Powahatan, an Indian chief. A famous story tells how she pleaded with her father to save John Smith's life. She married a colonist named John Rolfe, and visited England, where she died in 1617.

RICHES OF THE NEW WORLD

In 1589 Richard Hakluyt published *The Principal Voyages and Discoveries of the English Nation*. He had talked to captains, sailors and merchants about their adventures. His book encouraged England's leaders to look overseas for trade and for settlement.

Hakluyt's book told the story of Tudor exploration as an English epic. After defeating the Spanish Armada, Drake, Frobisher and Hawkins were heroes. Rich pickings from Spanish fleets filled the government's bank – one captured treasure cargo paid the Queen's expenses for a year.

However, as England's war with Spain continued through the 1590s, there were more disasters than triumphs. The English galleon *Revenge* was captured after a battle in which her captain, Sir Richard Grenville, died of his wounds. Raiding the Caribbean in 1595, Drake and Hawkins found Spanish defences stronger. Hawkins fell sick, and died. Drake failed in attacks on Puerto Rico and Panama, and in January 1596 he too died, from the disease dysentery.

Walter Raleigh still hoped to find gold in the New World. In 1595, he sailed to Guiana in South America to search for a 'golden city', the legendary El Dorado. Exploring the Orinoco River, he was "forced to lie in rain and weather, in the burning sun", but found no gold.

However, Raleigh wrote a book about his adventures that made South America seem like Paradise. Such tales made some people in England believe that the New World was ideal for settlement.

Privateers were warships paid for by rich nobles and merchants. English, French and Dutch privateers raided Spain's American empire.

England's queen was wary of sending her own ships on such raids so as not to anger the Spanish king. But she did not mind friends like the Earl of Cumberland (above right) paying for ships and crews.

▽ **Spanish treasure ships** at Nombre de Dios in Panama. Captured ships brought great riches. In 1592 Frobisher seized a Spanish ship carrying jewels, silks, ivory and porcelain. The cargo was worth 28 new galleons!

▷ **An English raid on a Spanish settlement in America.** Often the raiders joined forces with ex-slaves to attack towns.

▽ **An English ship attacks a Spanish treasure ship.**

◁ **The English sent expeditions to Asia as well as to America.**
● In 1586-88 Thomas Cavendish (left) made the second voyage round the world by an Englishman.
● In 1594 Sir James Lancaster sailed to the East Indies (Indonesia and Malaysia) and later set up several trading posts there.

AN EMPIRE BEGINS

Francis Bacon, the English scientist and statesman, wrote that human beings would "extend the power and dominion of the human race over the Universe." England was not strong enough to be a power in Europe so it developed an overseas empire.

A colony in America offered new lives to people with no future in England – such as landless farmers, and Catholics and Puritans seeking religious freedom. Merchants hoped to trade with the colonies. Settlers were sent out in groups to make their homes in 'New England'.

They found no gold, but enough land for all. The Indians lived by farming, fishing and hunting. The English did the same. They learned to grow new crops, and cut timber from the forests to build their homes. The French and Spanish also had settlements in North America, but only as outposts for traders, soldiers and priests. The English were the first Europeans to settle in big numbers. Their colonists founded the British Empire, and a future nation – the United States.

▽ **A map of Virginia** by John Smith, 1624.

▽ **The settlement at Jamestown, Virginia**, was the first successful English colony in America.
● Many of the 100 or so colonists (all men) died of hunger or sickness in the first years.
● Indians were at first helpful, but then tried to fight off the newcomers.
● Women joined the colony, and families learned how to grow their own food.

▽ **Tobacco growing** was the colonists' first trade. The English learned how to smoke from Indians, like Chief Tishcohan (below). By 1614 they were selling tobacco to England.

GLOSSARY

Armada Spanish fleet sent to invade England in 1588.

astrolabe navigation instrument for finding latitude (a ship's position north or south of the equator).

Aztecs people of Mexico conquered by Cortés.

backstaff improved navigation instrument for finding latitude.

cannon big gun, used by ships and on land.

chart map of ocean and coasts.

colony permanent settlement founded by a country overseas.

Company group of merchants sharing in trade ventures.

convoy group of ships sailing together for protection against attack.

corn (maize or sweetcorn), a food plant unknown in Europe before the exploration of America.

courtier person attending the king or queen at court.

El Dorado mythical city of gold in America.

fleet group of ships, usually under one person's command.

galleon sailing warship, built from the mid 1500s.

Incas people of Peru conquered by Pizarro.

Indians Columbus called the people of America Indians, believing he was in the 'Indies' (Asia).

merchant trader buying and selling overseas, by sending out ships or expeditions.

musket early hand-gun.

navigation finding and maintaining a ship's correct course or direction at sea.

New World European name for North and South America.

passage route or seaway, usually to a specific location.

pike weapon like a long spear with an axe-head.

pilot navigator of a ship, often a local sailor.

plantation large farm growing one crop, such as sugarcane or bananas.

slave person held captive and forced to work.

spices plants such as pepper, cinammon, ginger – used to flavour foods.

strait narrow channel of water, between two points of land.

tobacco plant of which dried leaves were smoked in pipes by American Indians. Pipe-smoking became popular in Europe.

▽ **Major regions of Tudor explorations.**

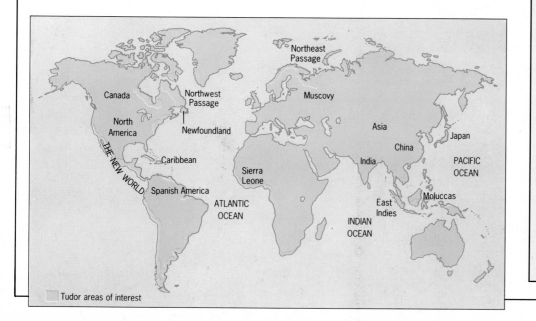

Tudor areas of interest

TIMECHART

1492 Columbus sails to America, the first European to do so since the Vikings.

1498 John Cabot dies seeking the Northwest Passage.

1508 Sebastian Cabot explores Hudson Bay.

1513 Balboa of Spain crosses Panama and sees the Pacific Ocean.

1519-22 Magellan's round the world expedition; one ship completes the voyage.

1553 Chancellor reaches the north coast of Russia.

1560s Hawkins makes slaving voyages between Africa and America.

1578 Frobisher makes last of three voyages to North America.

1577-80 Drake sails around the world.

1580s Davis explores the North American Arctic.

1585 Raleigh pays for colonists to sail to Roanoke Island in America.

1586-88 Cavendish's voyage around the world.

1587 Colony of Roanoke in America fails.

1589 Hakluyt publishes book about the English voyages.

1595 Raleigh explores South America, looking for El Dorado.

1607 Jamestown colony in America.

1620 *Mayflower* Pilgrims sail to America.

INDEX